A One-sided Always and Forever Love

A One-Sided Always and Forever Love

(How I Over Came It)

KIMBERLY LEWIS

iUniverse

A ONE-SIDED ALWAYS AND FOREVER LOVE
(HOW I OVER CAME IT)

iUniverse books may be ordered through booksellers or by contacting:

iUniverse
1663 Liberty Drive
Bloomington, IN 47403
www.iuniverse.com
1-800-Authors (1-800-288-4677)

Scripture taken from the King James Version of the Bible.

ISBN: 978-1-5320-1699-8 (sc)
ISBN: 978-1-5320-1701-8 (e)

Print information available on the last page.

iUniverse rev. date: 01/17/2018

PREFACE

I was really amazed at the number of broken homes/ marriages/relationships there were, of people that I knew personally. These people seem to be made for each other, so much in love. The breakups were so unreasonable. They would walk away still in love with their spouses. Not really knowing why or what happen or where did they go wrong. The revelation that the Lord gave me was so awesome I needed to share. I used my personal situation to explain what the Lord was saying in my own life, and praying that it may help others in their journey. Using my situation to guide and allow for adjustments to personalize to their circumstances.

INTRODUCTION

This story is about a young girl who thought she had met her soul mate and fell deeply in love. She carried the torch for over 30 years. Her sensible mine wanted to let go but she did'nt know how. Trying everything she could to move him out of her heart & mind. Prayers after prayers and to no prevail not knowing what was going wrong, she wanted to be free. Truly this person had gone on with his life and was not interested in her. She was stuck, but Jesus had a different plan, His plans & timing is so different than ours.

CONTENTS

MY STORY

'm driving home from work feeling very blue. Thinking I'm fed up with life, burned with love, doing without for so long, waiting for this special someone to come to his senses, wanting only this person, making it very hard for anyone else to fill the void that I am feeling, and totally unsatisfied with anything and everything.

The other day I got a call from his sister. She had not heard from him in a long time and was worried. The last phone number she had was not working. She asked me to find him on the internet. So, I did and gave her his number. She called him and then put a three-way call to me. I was not expecting her to call me back especially, with him on the phone. Normally, when I heard his voice my whole body, mind and soul would go through a serious change. It seemed like all of my problems would disappear. This time was different, the first thing that came out of my mouth was have you gotten your divorce? (He got married in 1981, and separated shortly after and never got a divorce. I don't date married men. (What you sow so shall you reap. Gal. 6:7). I respect the vows of marriage and I would not want someone to interfere with my marriage. So when I moved to the mid-west I felt as if I could not date him because he was still married, so I would always tell him to get a divorce, but, for whatever reason he didn't, before he moved out of state. It is now 2005). He answered yes. His response blew me away, "YES! And YOU HAVE NOT CONTACTED ME." I then asked "Well are you planning on getting remarried?" He said, I was thinking about it. Now, I'm finished with this conversation, assuming that he would marry the person he was living with. It cut so deep into my heart I could hardly stand it. Doing all that I could to do to keep my composure, not screaming, crying, continuing to breath and not exposing myself.

Now, I'm torn apart, totally distraught it all came to a head, and I found myself questioning God. "Why would you allow me to fall in love if we were not ever going to come together? Why would you allow me to love that deeply to only lose that person? Why would you allow me to have a relationship like that and it not come to a happy ending? Why would you allow me to meet the man of my dreams and we never be together? Why would you allow me to love and be loved like this and then tear it apart? Why would allow me to taste my dreams of true happiness and it not last? Why would you allow me to meet a man that fulfills all that I am looking for in a man, if he was never to be mine?"

Lord, I speak of this person almost daily as if he is sitting right here. I live my life as if he is a part of it right now. Every decision that I make, I analyze it as if he is helping me make it or asking what would he do? I live my life as if he just went to the store and will be right back or is simply gone out of town. I haven't seen him for years. I have not talked to him it seems like in forever. I've pushed away good men I met because I felt as if he was my husband and will be returning soon. I never gave them a chance; they could not measure up to him. They weren't tall enough or too tall. They weren't big enough or too big, or they weren't educated enough or entirely too deep. They weren't romantic enough or to mushy, their conversation wasn't interesting. They weren't manly enough and a push over and I could not ever respect them. <u>I wanted a man to take control without being controlling</u>. We wouldn't have any thing in common. Being intimate was a totally different issue with a whole new group of comparisons. They were constantly under comparison to him and none could compare. They wondered what was going on. This invisible person was preventing me from having a good relationship. I've played myself down to keep any one from wanting to talk to me (I kept men away on purpose). I would always say "I didn't have a problem getting a man just getting rid of them." Therefore they never had a fair chance.

Those, whom I gave a chance, would be only be for practice. I learned how to treat and take care of them, I did things that the average woman would not do in this day and age, such as: I loved to cook; there was always a hot fresh meal cooked to perfection, there was always a steaming hot tub of water to take a bath and a good body massage if necessary when they came home from work. Little things like that, I loved doing. Which spoiled them, but they weren't the one it was intended for. I was totally emerged in being the perfect wife, mother and also holding a career. They would fall in love and I didn't, they were really puzzled. When I perfected my skill it was time for them to leave, of course they didn't want to go. When I was trying to get rid of them often things would get dangerous, I'm not naturally a violent person, but I will defend myself. You see he satisfied me mentally and physically. There was nothing about him that I did not adore. For my man, my prayer was Lord if there had to be something wrong with him, let him have big feet.

When we were together, we seem to be on the same wave link (soul ties). We seem to be thinking the same thoughts. We gave each other their freedom and we would miss each other at the same time. When he crossed my mind or I started missing him, he would show up. Even when he was out of town he would call or I would get a letter in the mail.

I needed to get this person out of my life even though he was not in it. He's truly gone on with his life. I felt his presence and he was not there. He was probably not thinking about me at all. I could feel it when something was going on with him, good or bad, happy or sad. Somehow I knew he had an issue. I would be commissioned to pray for him. It seem like I was always praying for him. I told my pastor that I was tired of praying for him. I could not stop thinking about him. He was always on my mind. It has been about 30 years now. When I hear his voice my world still stops. When I see a picture my heart still beats harder. When I look into his face or think about him I still glow like I'm fifteen years old. People would tell me, that I was literally glowing when I would think about him. This doesn't make any sense. I still think of moments that we had together. Memories are as fresh as if it happened yesterday. Even bad memories still haunt me. Every mistake I made I still cry about them. Every argument still hurts. It has been over 20 years sense we were a couple. I can't stop this. I need help. So I decided to emerge myself in the Lord. People would tell me that I had to break soul ties. *(Jehovah Nakah, Isaiah 58:11. And the Lord shall guide you continually, and satisfy thy soul in drought, and make fat thy bones: and thou shall be like a watered garden, and like a spring of water, whose waters fail not).*

I did what I was thought to do to break soul ties. But he is still here in my mind & heart.

(I prayed Lord! please take him out of my heart & mend my broken heart. Please release him out of my mind and life. Lord, please give me my heart back. I'm tired of being alone; I'm tired of him unknowingly running my life. I want my life back. I want to have control of my own mind. I want him out of my system. I would like to let him go. What else is it that I need to do? How do I stop comparing others to him? Lord, I need your help. I've done all that I know to do to remove him from my life.)

Always personalize your prayers.

THE REVELATION

n the mist of asking these questions and voicing my concerns to the Lord, I received a revelation from the Lord. I heard the Lord's say in a very small and calm voice saying:

"ASK FOR YOUR LOVE BACK"

I thought, with love always come joy, peace and happiness. Without love there is no joy, peace or happiness. You are unbalanced not whole. For a relationship to work you have to be whole. It takes two whole people to make a whole, successful relationship. Spiritually this type of love is very intimate an unconditional love. It's a special type of love, an everlasting love. No one else can satisfy you or make you feel real. You know beyond a shadow of a doubt that you are destined to be together. With this type of love that you are willing to let them go if it makes them happy. You would sacrifice your own happiness for theirs. Being with them you feel that you can accomplish anything, it is as though things would just fall into place. All that doesn't fall into place is okay. You don't mind not having the things that you want because being with them is enough.

When you meet someone else, and you can't understand why things or your relationships is not working. One or both of you are not whole. We often realize that we gave them our hearts and ask the Lord for our heart back or to mend your broken heart, but you need love, to balance yourself in life.

When you first fall in love, often times you are very young. In my grandparents day people got married at the age of 12 and 13. If you were unmarried at the age of 16 girls were considered an old maid. Those marriages would often last for a life time. They marry their first true loves.

When you first fall in love, you give your all to that relationship. You sing songs (what is spoken in the atmosphere shall come to pass), that have important words, words that haunt you the rest of your life. Such as; "I will love you always,"; "Always and Forever." "There will never be another." "For once in my life."; "You are the only one." You write poems & letters. You dream dreams, make plans and say things. You have expectations of what you want to happen. You pour your most intimate part of you into the relationship. You vision your future with this person. I'm speaking of your first real love, which comes for people at different ages, usually at a very young age. This person you never really forget. You keep them in the back of your mind, throughout life. For whatever reason when things fall apart for a split second their face will flash across your mind.

I found myself, disgusted, depressed, full of anger, unsatisfied, and with a loss of all hope. Without love, and joy happiness was a thing of the past. Most, of my youth I was exceedingly happy. I could find joy in anything. I was always bubbly and full of energy, always looking for good time with good innocent fun. Enjoying myself everywhere I went. I was often called the life of the party. When I entered a room the fun began. Friends were everywhere, I never met a stranger. Always encouraging others in whatever situation they were experiencing. My sister once said, "I don't like going places with you, because when you walk in you draw attention, and I just want to walk in, have a seat and not be seen." I believe it was the Lord's joy that place that into my personality. (Presently my personality has changed). I found people young and old, from all warps of life wanting to talk to me and be in my presence. I found most of my closer friends were my peer's parents. After talking to me they left at peace with a better understanding. God placed in me a form of peace that surpasses understanding, at a very young age. (... *the peace of God which passeth all understanding... Phil. 4:7*) I learned at a young age not to worry about things that I could not change and change the thing that I could. He always empowered me to have the things I needed, to accomplish what needed to be accomplished. That kept me at peace. And I shared that peace (so I thought) with everyone who came around me. My family didn't understand how or why I didn't worry about anything. They would make statements saying "I worried all night." I would say "why?" Not worrying would allow me to hear from God. (*Cast your cares unto God... Ps.55:22*) I didn't know at the time that it was God speaking to me. My mother would call it "Her first mine". So I utilize that peace at all times. God always came through. (*He's faithful just trust in Him. Ps.111:7*) I felt that I was special. I felt that I had special powers. That whatever I wanted it would come.

When I would be down to my last dime, someone would come and give me money that they owed me. I'm a cosmetologist (hair stylist), some people in my community would not always have all or any of the money to pay me. I would take payment of most kinds and promissory notes. My family would often get upset with me because of the way I handled my business. But I felt that they would pay me or the Lord would bless me. I did not worry about it. If they didn't pay me, I would consider it a blessing and give it to them. *(He who hath pity upon the poor lendeth unto the Lord; Proverbs 19:17)* (Since then I have learned do not to lend what I cannot afford to give away. I've learned to balance it. I guess that was what I was doing all the time. But God always came through.

See before you get in the word, if you have the right kind of heart (intentions) the principles of the Lord would automatically come through without you realizing it. The two biblical principles I learned was "Do unto others what you would have others do unto you." and *("What so ever a man soweth so shall he reap. Gal. 6:7).* So I was very careful of the things that I would do to others. What you do to others will come back to you. The seeds that you plant will grow a harvest. Good or Bad. I truly did not want bad things to come on to me. That was one of the ways I stayed in peace. I didn't notice when my peace left. My mother died. Peace left gradually; just as this relationship seem too have dissolved.

As it dissolved, so did my happiness. I tried to continue as normal but everything seemed to be falling apart. I didn't know what was happening. I could not be satisfied in any area of my life. The men that I met were not satisfying. I only wanted to be bothered with them when I wanted to be. My family seemed to not act as a family should. My friends begin to scatter. Along with normal life changes it seemed that I started making the wrong decisions. I got where I didn't care. I found myself floating from person to person and from situation to situation with no direction. My family was not cooperating. Nothing made me happy. Nothing was satisfying. I used food, cigarettes, and drink to pass the days away. Happiness had left the house. (My Temple) I praise the Lord that I didn't have an addictive personality, and didn't like drugs and alcohol. There is no telling where I would be. Food became my drug (addiction). You cannot expect for food, drink, drugs, or people to make you happy. The Lord (Jehovah Shalom, God of Peace,) is the only being that can help you in those areas. I learned that some people will plot/plan for your demise and follow thru, with the help of satan. People will only walk so far with you before they leave or stop. But the Lord will not leave you or forsake you *(...so I will be with the: I will not fail thee, nor forsake thee. Joshua 1:5)*. He is always there. He is only a call away, whether your phone is working or not. It doesn't require an electric outlet to contact Him. He has a divine connection. He understands your heart, if you feel that you cannot pray your heart (Holy Spirit within) can & will pray for you. The Lord doesn't look at the outside of you or what you are doing or have done. He looks into your heart. Satan can and will stir up the atmosphere and make things seem different from what you intended, but the Lord knows what your intentions were/are from the beginning. He is always forgiving and understanding full of Grace and Mercy. He can bring happiness in your life & He will. Always seek Him first in all that you do *(But seek ye first the kingdom of God, and His righteousness; and all these things will be added unto you. Matt. 6:33).* You will find joy, peace, happiness & love with Him. I praise the Lord for Him being who He is in my life, loving me first *(We love because He loved us first. 1 John 4:19).*

The revelation that the Lord gave me, to ask for my love back, was very encouraging, and a real eye opener, it really refreshed my soul. The importance of possessing your own love is wonderful, being able to choose a mate without judging. It gave me a different outlook of people; it helps me to understand why some people can't understand what happen in their relationships. You go a lifetime not knowing why they could not love or be loved. I've always wanted what I want, including people there are particular types of body styles and looks, if you didn't fall in this range I didn't give you conversation. I knew that I would get tired of them after so long, so why go through the changes. It was a very narrow range, this revelation help me to see people as they are and appreciate the qualities that they have.

But Lord it's been 30 years. A lot of time has gone by. I feel as though I could be so much further along with my life. I planned to be married with lots of children, big home, a grandchild or two and lifelong happiness. I wanted to pursue a famous career. I knew I could bring home the bacon, fry it in a pan and make my man still feel like a man. By now my house would be a home. But instead there is nothing, none of my plans came to pass. Years have passed by.

Throughout all of this I became bitter, mean, cold, uncaring, suspicious, untrusting, hateful, and unforgiving. I want the carefree, loving gentle, compassionate person that

I was back, the person that always looked at the best part of a situation instead of the worst part. A half full glass verses a half empty glass. I had to find myself again. I had to be made whole. Pieces of me was scattered all over the place.

FORGIVENESS

In finding myself again I found me having to learn to forgive. In forgiving I had to find out who, what, when, where and how to forgive. I was never a very forgiving person. I always thought that what goes around comes around, again do unto others what you would have done unto you. It will come back to you good, bad, or ugly. I tried not to do anything wrong or evil to anyone. I felt that God would get you back. And I tried to give God the revenge. I thought if God gets you back, you have been gotten good. God could do a much better job than I could. (I have since learned that God forgives everyone, even those who hurt you.) But, I would tell others that, "I always pay my debts, I may be slow, but I pay them and I owe you". I really meant God will handle it. So, I was careful of the things I did and said. I felt like if you did or said something to me intensionally you meant it. Therefore, I did not accept your apology and I did not forgive you. I had to understand that sometimes things looked intensionally, that was not at all, and people don't think like I do, their values morals and motives are different. People often do before they think and they don't count the cost.

Now I've come to realize that forgiveness is for me not the other party. Un-forgiveness is a bitter root for illness.

In all, I first had to forgive myself for all the expectations of happiness with this person and limiting happiness to him only. Because I'm not happy, the joy that I always had on a daily basis was gone, (I don't know when it left), and peace had abandoned me. I had to forgive myself for allowing many good relationships to slip away without trying to maintain them. I didn't want to be in a relationship that was not with him. I could not give the love, the type of love it took to hold a relationship together. You cannot give what you don't have. I gave it away a long time ago. I didn't realize that God had others that could make me happy and adore me and I didn't give them a chance. I forgive myself for just being ignorant, picky and spoiled.

I then forgave him for not meeting my expectations. For not being my knight in shining armor, my superman that I always thought he was. I had to forgive him for not rescuing me from the evilness that had overtaken me and my life, for not rescuing me from the people only that lived, to make my life unbearable. (It seemed that their mission in life was to make life for me miserable. For this I had to forgive him also.) For not paying attention when he felt that I was in trouble and not following up on what he felt. (I was in a relationship where the person would not leave or leave me alone which resulted in me moving to the Midwest), I know that he must have felt something was wrong at least he had always sensed things before. For not loving me the way I wanted him to, for not fulfilling my dreams with him, and seeming not to care. For not truly loving me the way I loved him. I forgave him for not making me his one and only. I then sent his love back to him.

I realized that others had loved me. I also have to send love back to those whose love that I was holding. I had to send their love back, back individually, to release them. I simply said aloud in prayer and in my heart,

("Lord forgive me for using these people, (I named them) will you please return the love of theirs that I am holding, release them please. I'm sending them their love back, the love that is holding them that is making them unhappy and unsatisfied with life. Lord, please release those that I have forgotten, missed, or just didn't realized. Thank you Jesus". Amen).

REVELATION 2

hen I heard the Lord say,

"ASK FOR YOUR TIME WASTED BACK"

I thought of all the things that I wanted to accomplish in all of that time. Places I wanted to go. I eventually got mixed up with some of the wrong types (shady) of people and trapped in horrible situations, allowing their bad decisions include me. People who lived their lives to destroy mine, I experienced some things that really weren't a part of my personality, while depending on these people thinking they had my best interest at heart. Boy was I wrong, Praise the Lord God, through it all, God was there taking what satan meant for evil and turning it into good (... *He hath requited me evil for good. Samuel 25:21)*. It could have been so much worse, but God never left me nor did He forsake me. I learn a lot about people. I praise God (Jehovah Nakah, He who guides me,) for the strength, and the strong mind that God gave me. The ability to think fast on my feet, the sharpness of my thoughts, this really saved my life on numbers occasions. I thank God for the ability to not get involved in the things I saw, but to learn from what I saw. I thank God for being able to look at both sides of an equation, & the ability to reading between lines. During this time God showed me and taught me many things about life. I experienced things that I did not know existed. I learned to trust Him, when I did not know Him. I think that God will allow you to experience things without getting involved, so you can guide people in the right direction. The time was not so much wasted but life lessons, ministering to people and myself, teaching, & training and bringing up my children in the way to go.

One of the Pastor's under the umbrella of our church once said that the Lord taught him how to minister to drug addicted people and he never took drugs before in his life. I wonder if he experienced drugs without using them. God has many ways to teach people to minister to his people. Through my experiences I have been able to unofficially minister to people. Again what satan meant for evil, God turn it to good.

But as for my life, it seemed to be put on hold. During that time I had two wonderful children. I always knew that if I had this person to back me (stand with me or catch me if I fall) I could do anything. Not realizing that the Lord was backing me all the time and His backing was solid, and unchanging. At the time of the revelation I felt very bad about the years that I waited for this man, to fulfill my dreams. He had asked me to marry him. I waited thinking that someday it would come to pass. Though many men had asked me to marry them they weren't what I wanted. I did not want to be tied up when this man came back.

During this time I slowly gained weight, allowed my health

to go down. I lost interest in caring for myself. Let myself go. I did only what was needed to do daily, but that was it. I allowed myself to become unattractive. Being in the field of cosmetology and not doing what I knew to do to maintain my attractiveness. I didn't want them to fall in love. Because I knew that I would only use them and never love them enough for a relationship to withstand. I never had a problem getting men. My problem was getting rid of them. At that time in my life I thought of men as toys. I didn't want to play on their emotions. I was very straight forward on how I felt, but people thought because I treated them kindly that I did not mean what I said. They would think that they were special and that they could change me. But like I said earlier, I found something about them that did not impress me or just was not good enough for me and turn me off.

I then built this invisible wall around me, which did not allow anyone to see or come in into my world and it covered me where I really could not be seen. I was simply protecting my empty heart. It worked so well that men treated me as though I was not there.

Being from down south men there were courteous and helpful. It did not matter if they knew you or not. I never carried groceries or open doors (if there was a male around). Mid-western men were different. They expected you to do for them. There have been occasions when I would be approaching a door at the same time as a man and he would literally stand there and wait on me to open the door. If I wasn't careful he would walk in before me.

One of my girlfriends went home with me down south; we stopped to get gas on the way. Just as I stopped I noticed that there was a car and a truck full of men at the gas station. It was early evening; it looked as if they were just getting off from work. I looked at her and said we may not have to pump any gas. Before I finished saying it, three men ran to my car and one asked me if he could pump my gas for me. Not wanting anything just honored to do it. She was flabbergasted. She had never seen anything like that before.

Where I rented an apartment in Mid-west, parking was on the street. One morning I was running late for work. Just as I came out of the house the sanitation truck (picking up trash) was parked in the street one car behind me. As I ran out of the house approaching my van, the driver was getting in his truck. He looked in my face, waited until I got in my van and pulled up just enough to block me in. I got so angry I screamed "why would you block me in?" You see I'm in a hurry. I told him how wrong he was and if I had been of another race he would not have done that.

Another incident, I needed gas and pulled into a gas station. There was a truck in front of me, so I pulled up as close to him in line as I could. I went in the gas station to pay cash for my gas. While I was in line inside, the truck finished pumping and left, then I notice a car backing in front of my van. I then went to the door and told him I'm paying for my gas. He then pulled off. I paid for my gas, and as I'm getting into the van another car started backing up in front of me. I screamed what are you doing? The guy finished backing and got out of his car, walked up to my van & asked me what did I say? I told him and said that I'm about to get my gas that I already paid for. He then got back in to his car and started cleaning his car out his car (literally) then he got out and opened his back door and cleaned out the back seat and floor.

He put the trash in the can and walked up to my window and said if I had not said what I said he would have moved. I waited for a moment, he still didn't move then I flipped open my phone. When he saw me on the phone then he quickly moved; he did not know who I was calling.

Men would not make eye contact so they would not have to speak or speak quickly, they would turn their heads look in another direction. This would happen in all settings, church, on the street, at the store or just anywhere, whether they knew me or not, and caring a conversation with me would be out of the question.

I had to remember it was not the person, it is the spirit guiding them or surrounding me, at that moment, and they are being used. It is not flesh and blood but principalities that I'm dealing with. *(For we wrestle not against flesh and blood, but against principalities, against powers, against the rulers of darkness of this world, against spiritual wickedness in high places Eph. 6:12)*

It had gotten ridiculous; I began to wander what is going on. Now I'm older, I should be getting more respect. I'm losing respect for men quickly. I was beginning to think of men as being dogs, low life creatures with no manners, at least the men in the mid-west. (All Mid-Western men are not like that, it's that I haven't met them yet!)

Thirty years of my life is gone and here's where I end up. With the Lord saying Ask for your time wasted back. I thought Lord it's been 30 years. Lord You will really restore/ returned 30 years to my life. *(And I will restore to you the years that the locust hath eaten, and the cankerworm, and the caterpillar, and the palmerworm, my great army which I sent among you. Joel 2:25)*

("Lord I ask for the time wasted back, time that I have lost being without love or a meaningful relationship. The years of loneliness (with or without a person in my life) waiting for him to returned to me.")

I began imagining what is going to be restored. I thought my 30 years being restored; "I'll get the opportunity to minister with real knowledge." If I only knew then what I know now, but God has always given me common, spiritual, street sense and discernment. I could always sense something wrong or something not quite right in a situation. I always read between the lines. I read people very well. I think he gives discernment to everyone; the difference is that I always paid attention, listen, followed up and spoke my mind. Often I read more into it, than people wanted revealed. God always spoke to me about what was going on. My mom always called it her first mine. He would speak directly to me and with so much authority, and I jumped to the occasion.

GOD SPEAKS TO ME

*T*he first time I remember God speaking to me directly. My mother had been sick and was home from the hospital she was doing well and told me to get out of the house for a few minutes, so I went visit to a girlfriend. We were listening to music and dancing. Suddenly the Lord said "GO HOME KIM". Without thinking I jumped up and said I got to go home and started running home. Just as I got in the house and stepped into the kitchen, my mother was opening a kitchen cabinet door and the entire cabinet came off the wall coming down on her. Being taller than my mother I caught the cabinet over her head. That totally blew our minds. The cabinet was not an old cabinet, nor was it loose or rigidity. Mom was speechless she just turned and went back to bed. It had to be God to send me home at that exact second to catch the cabinet before it fell on her. Surprisingly nothing in the cabinet hit her.

Another incident, my friend always complained about my driving. We were together and I was driving on a street that had the complete right away. It was a small community where all of the cross side streets had stop signs. I was diving at a comfortable speed. Suddenly I heard the Lord say "KIM STOP". I hit the brakes coming to a streaking halt. My friend looked at me and screamed what are you doing? Before he could finish the sentence a car ran the stop sign at a very high speed right in front of us. He would have run into the side of my car, right where he was sitting. It would have been a terrible crash, judging by the speed of the other driver. Needless to say he never complained about my driving again.

With the Lord telling me to ask for the time wasted back I had no problem doing it.

(*"Lord it has been 30 years and I'm unhappy with my life, You told me to ask for my time that I wasted back. Lord please return my time. Return the things that I did not achieve that I would have during this time, return the things that I lost, return the things that I missed, and double the inheritance that I missed during this time."*)

The Lord then gave me more things to call back.

CALL BACK

I call back all the words that I spoke into this relationship to return. You know the Lord formed the world with his words. By simply saying "Let there be..." *(...and God said let there be light and there was light... Gen. 1:3, 6, & 14,)* and it came to pass. Words have consequences. You set a course for your life with the words you speak. *(Death and Life are in the power of the tongue... Proverbs 18:21)* When your words are in your heart it, becomes a powerful force. Your words affect you more than anything or anyone else words can. You then work towards bring them to pass. The words you place into the atmosphere they come to pass. That is why it is so important watch what you say. Life and death is in the power of the tongue. You should always speak blessings not curses life not death. When you say things about people, don't get upset when they fulfill it. "You Dog." When he/she starts cheating or doing ungodly things remember you call them a dog. When you call your child stupid don't wonder why he/she can't or won't learn or do crazy things. Words are important always. "I can't find a job". Then your searches come to a standstill.

"I'm broke", then you can't seem get a dollar or keep any money. "I'll never love another". No one else can satisfy you. We sing songs, the words of that song have meaning, and they too affect our lives also. Speak good words, "my child is a genius". "I have a wonderful spouse. I'm wealthy, rich, a child of God and He loves me." "My job is in the making." "My best days are yet to come." "Each day gets better and better." "My children are very intelligent." You see your words are very important in whatever circumstance you use them.

(Lord, I call back the meaning that I gave words that I spoke into this relationship. The love and meanings I poured into words and the relationship. The meanings that I made the words in my life, the expectations I had in building this relationship, I erase the anger, mistrust, loneliness that came along being without him. These things I asked in Jesus Name!)

This is just some of the changes that came along within those 30 yrs.

I call back all of the: I love you's I said in his presence, on the phone, in a song, in my thoughts, on paper, in letters or anywhere. These things I asked in Jesus Name!

I call back the desires I had for him only, his level headedness of his thoughts when a decision needed to be made. I desired the way he gently took control of situations without strong arming the problem. His calming presence (when he was around I felt safe and unthreatened & secure, I could relax; exhale). I desired his touch and his touch only. I desired to hear his voice, the way it felt to be in his arms, the gentleness and softness when he held me, the contentment that I received from him mentally and physically, the way he always showed up when I needed someone, the careful way he chose his words of comfort, the softness of his lips when we kissed. The strength and control he had over every muscle in his body. I desired the way he romanced me and made me feel like a woman. I desire all of his caring ways. He seemed to know what I needed, how I needed it and exactly when, even when I didn't know myself. I felt that knew all about me. I felt if he took the time to know all about me and supplied my needs, wants, wishes and desires within reason, that he really loved me and I desired that type of love. I desire the quiet moments when he just held me without saying word. I desired the caring way he took care of me when I was sick or just didn't feel good. I loved the way he handled finances and entrusting me to do the right thing. I desired the way he always wanted to provide for me and mine. I desire the way he satisfied me mentally. I call back the memories of these desires that I attached to him believing that only he could provide these things, (and no other could), which blocked or hindered another from being loved by me. I know I am spoiled. In the Name of Jesus!

I recall all of the plans that I had for us. I call back my plans for our wedding (I had designed my wedding gown), for our family, purchasing our home. All of the children I planned to have, traveling together, with all of the little things done together, such as picking out furniture, choosing what neighborhoods we were to live in, silver ware & china. Living that fairy tale life full of love, joy, and peace and living happily ever after. I remove the person that I placed in those plans with me, and I will still have those plans with my husband that God has ordained for me to have. The man that God made to fit me. *(...and then the Lord God said. It is not good for man to live alone; I will make man an help meet for him Gen. 2:18).* Please return and bring these things In The Name Of Jesus!

I call back all of the jesters we made and pet names that we had for each other. In having enjoying each other, I want to give it to the man that you have for me Lord.

I call back all the dreams of us being together and the accomplishments we were to make as one, his children that I dreamed of having. I need my dreams back that I shared with him Lord in the name Jesus.

I call back all of the memories of the walks, dates, moments we spent together. These things keep him in my mind and soul. Lord I need not to keep him there.

I call back the visions of us spending our entire life together or at least giving it a try. We never got the chance to try it.

One of my prayers is "Lord I call back all the things that I made permanent, to paste this relationship together". I know now that I need to remove the person that I place there and replace them with the one you have for me. The one that you made to fit me.

The Lord is still giving me things to recall, to ask to come back to me. It took years to build a relationship it does not go away in a few minutes, or overnight. You have to realize what they are first. There is nothing wrong with the things that I called back or ask for back from the Lord, I need to place them with the one that God has for me. I just need to focus on God's will. Let God's will be done." *(...thy Kingdom come. Thy will be done on earth as it is in Heaven... Matt. 6:9-11).*

HOW I MET HIM

*I*n the early fall of my freshman year in High School one of my closes girlfriend came to me tell me about this guy that just moved into the neighborhood. She knew that I would like him. He lived up the street from me. As she described him, I thought to myself I know that a man with that description, didn't live on my street and I had not seen him. She really wanted me to meet him. He seems to be all I wanted in a young man physically and kind of cute also.

During the school year my girlfriends and I were together constantly. During the summer I worked and lived with my uncle learning how to do hair. This guy moved into the neighborhood during the summer. School started and he rode the same bus that we rode. But, still I had never seen him. Living down South the days were warm on into December.

One warm day I stood on her carport waiting on her to go walking. And from behind me there were a noise. When I turned around there stood this Adonis. About 6 feet tall, 34 inch waist, 48 inch chest 17 inch biceps, 28 inch thighs, nicely bow legged, browned skinned, nice afro, wearing a muscle shirt, hip hugger jeans with bell bottoms and converse gyms shoes. He startled me, but soon I went into action. As I gazed into his brown eyes (now turning blue), I thought who is this? This body is unbelievable (home grown). I then started to walk around him. Every muscle seemed to be carved into place. I circled him at least 3 times looking him up and down (checking him out completely). We had not said a word at this point. I could tell he was getting nervous. He folded his arms and placed one hand under his chin. Not knowing what to do with himself, finally we were face to face and I asked him where had he been all of my life. It left him speechless. Just then my girlfriend came outside and introduced us. I think that he had the deepest voice that I had ever heard in a young man. It growled at me and my whole body trembled.

We became very good friends, but He was dating someone else. Our friendship became closer and closer. We became inseparable. I gave him very sound advice dealing with his girlfriend. You could say I kept them together for a while. We liked lots of the same things. We especially enjoyed each other company. Our friendship grew and grew into a lovely relationship. I am a romantic by nature. Eventually we became a couple.

THE PICTURE

rowing up I had a group of girlfriends, being girls we often talked about boys, and what we were going to do with our lives, who we were going to marry, the boys we liked, & the famous people that we were totally in love with. I have always had a very vivid imagination. I would vision things and often I would draw what I saw. Dealing with what our husbands would look like. I decided to draw a picture. I could draw very well, but, I could not draw hands and feet. Therefore, I drew a man standing in the water at the beach, with his hands on his hip in swimming trunks. I must have been in the six or seventh grade. I like the picture so much I placed it on my wall in my bedroom. I looked at that picture every day & dreamed about the man in it. You could say that <u>I fell in love with the man in that picture.</u>

Our neighborhood was in essence a small neighborhood. Everybody knew each other. In some cases there were a lot of people related. The kids played together mostly in blocks. Whatever block, street you lived on or church you attended were most of your best friends. We would often play softball, kick ball, dodge ball or Frisbee on empty lots or behind a group of houses. One sunny day we were playing Frisbee behind a group of houses. One of the houses was not occupied and the grass had grown up a little. The way we played Frisbee was we had a center line with two groups of players. You had to throw the as deep into the other teams playing field as possible. Where ever you caught the Frisbee you had to throw it back from there. He had just ran down the Frisbee, caught it and threw it. Feeling a little winded he bent over to catch his breath. Then he stood up with his hands on his hip standing in the tall grass. When I turned and looked up, he looked exactly like the picture I had drowned years ago. I thought that I had found my soul mate.

The more I got to know him the deeper I fell in love. I really appreciated his spiritual upbringing. His, what we call his Home Training, the way he treated girls/women or people in general. He was very respectful and courteous. With his personality I found his faults minimal. I FOUND THE MAN IN MY PICTURE!!

HOW I LOST HIM

My parents divorced when I was very young and like so many fathers he didn't play a role in my life. My mother did all for me. I wanted to be a cosmetologist all of my life. My uncle and aunt was cosmetologist. They both had begun training me in the field but, I worked with my uncle as an apprentice for approximately 5 yrs., he played a larger role in training me. I started at the tender age of 13, my summer between my 8th grade and 9th grade year. I worked each weekend and all summers. One of the first salons that I worked with him in, my father got his hair done in that salon. He told me if I really wanted to do hair that he would help me and get a building for a salon. After I graduated from high school I started cosmetology school but, I began school in the middle of the term and needed my books, uniform, and kit which totaled about $200. The grant checks were disbursed at the beginning of the term. I remembered what my father said, and decided to ask him for the money. I had never asked my father for anything.

I went to his house to ask him for the money. My father

had remarried and his wife did not like my sister or myself and always tried to keep us apart from our father. She was there as I was talking to him and of course she had to add her input. We had words. I explain to him what I needed and what I needed it for and approximately when I would return it. He proceeded to tell me to ask my mother to put in on her credit card and he would pay her back. I explained that I thought that my mother had taken care of us all of our life without his help and that he told me that he would help. I was not asking him to give me anything but to loan it to me and I would pay him back. He then pull out a large roll of money and fished through it, to find a $10 bill and handed it to me. I then gave him his money back and told him if that was all that he could give me then to keep it, it would not help me. I was totally distraught. I left in tears.

I had a very small clientele that were sick or shut in and I would go to their homes and do their hair. I had two sisters scheduled for that day one of them was blind, I went to their home. Being upset it seemed to take a long time to finish them.

On my way home I remembered that a girlfriend was having a birthday party so I decided to go to it, hoping that the party could cheer me up. As I turned on her street is saw my boyfriend's car. The closer I got to the car I noticed that a female was sitting on it. I recognized her she was an old friend of his family which I knew, but my friends at the party did not know her. I was hurt and angry. Angrier because it was very disrespectful to me for him to bring another woman to this party, beside it just didn't look right. The two most important men in my life had betrayed me on the same day.

Our relationship was different than most, we always

remain friends no matter what. I knew at that moment that it was over for us as a couple, but our friendship I assumed that would continue. I pulled up and spoke to them. I got out of the car and opened his trunk to get a wine cooler there was only two left (he would buy me a case of wine coolers and himself a case of beer). I took both of the wine coolers and told her that I wanted to borrow him for a moment; she knew we were a couple. She said go head. I asked him to get in the car. I wanted to make the block. One of the first things that I said is I know that it was over for us, but I have a problem I need to borrow some money and I will pay him back when I got my grant check about three weeks away. "Busted", I thought that he would be vulnerable. Instead, the conversation got heated, one word lead to another. He asked me "what I was doing running the street that time of night." I said "that did not matter, will you loan me the money?" He then stated "any lady would not be running the street that time of night." Then I said "what is that sitting on your car?" He said something smart, I said "I will pour this whole cooler on you," and I did. He said "Do you want to fight?" I was so hurt and angry I said "You are mighty right" I pulled off the street and jumped out of the car. He jumped out and ran, I drew back as if I was going to throw the bottle at him then he stopped and asked me not to throw it. He began to explain what happen for him to bring her in my neighborhood. So we talked for a moment. I did not buy what he was saying but I wanted and needed the money. He proceeded to say, "You are a jealous something aren't you, "I said how would you, feel if you had rolled up on me and some man was sitting on my car and drinking your beer"? He said jokingly "it was kind of cozy wasn't it" that threw my into a brain overload I blinked out, my instinct took over, and I slapped him so hard. He says that he saw daylight at mid-night. At first I didn't know what happen, I heard a loud noise, when I opened my eyes he was standing there holding his face, glaring down at me. I didn't know what he was going to do, but he just walked off.

We stayed away from each other for two days. In the meantime my car started acting up. So I found him and asked him would he check out my car and what about the money? With this very serious look on his face he said "You mean to tell me that you almost broke my jaw and have nerve to ask me for some money." I knew at that point that our relationship was completely over. So I left.

I had grown very close to his mother and told her what had happen, she told me that the old friend had ran away from home and her mother was looking for her, which lined up with his story.

Less than a week went by, on Saturday morning by I heard a knock at my door and when I opened it, it was him asking me "what was wrong with my car?" He took the car and repaired it. At that moment our relationship shifted, it now had a new meaning. Plans were being made, a future was discussed. We were looking an apartment and put furniture on layaway. I saw a new side of him a more responsible and more loving side. I felt as if he woke up and found me. I felt that he wanted to take the next step. All of my dreams were coming true. A growth spurt has taken place in our relationship. I felt more important to him, surely the "QUESTION" was going to be next.

I got a call from his mother to come to her house, of course I went. Before I could tell her that we were back together. She had a message for him (they were on bad terms and was not speaking at that moment). She said that his sisters needed help, that they both worked two jobs and needed him to help with his nephew. And he had to go there. The only problem was that they lived in the Mid-west. She had already purchased his ticket and he was to leave Friday (today's Wednesday) and she wanted me to tell him. I could not believe my ears, I said WHAT! We were finally getting our life together. I didn't know what to do, I could not disobey her, but I didn't want him to go. I decided that I would let him make the decision.

When I told him what she said, I didn't know what to expect. First he had this frown on his face, then he smiled, then he frowned again. His first word was okay, I said okay. You are going! He said yes, I will send for you and your daughter. I'll get a job and send for you. I felt like my world had started dissolving before my eyes and it was nothing I could do to stop it. I could not believe that he was going to go. I knew in my heart that I would not see him again. He did all that he could do to convince me that he would send for me and it would not be a long time. But I just knew it was over. My heart cracked and broke; all of my purpose was destroyed. I could not believe what I was hearing, I got weak, I felt faint, my tears took life of their own, & I had no control, I could not find words to say. OMG! I knew it was the end.

We had to prepare for his trip, it was the end of December and it was cold in the mid-west, and like summer down south. He needed warm clothes and boots etc... the next day we shopped and spent as much time together as we could. My mother didn't know what was happening so she didn't understand why he was hanging around so much.

The next day was the day of his departure. I took him to

the bus station. That had to be the worst day of my life and to this day it still is. We hardly said a word, all he kept saying was "don't cry" I should have cried right then and there maybe he would not have left. But I tried to hold it as long as I could; finally they called his for the passengers to line up for his bus. I was torn up and I said "I have to go, I could not breath, my eyes were full and hurting, my heart was cracking, and my legs began to wobble. My head was about to explode, my hands was shaking. My whole system was off balance. I couldn't speak or think, my mind was racing, scared and completely out of control. I said "I cannot watch you get on that bus and leave." And I ran off, before I got to my car tears were flowing and I could not stop them. That day I found out that God knew how to drive. I don't know how I got home. I could not see, I could not think, I could not function it still hurts as I am writing about 30 yrs. later. It's sad, I'm crying as I type.

We kept in touch for a while. Finally, he asked me to come, but he was living with his sisters in a two bedroom apartment. I want him to get us a place, I had a child and we need at least a bedroom for her.

In the meantime my mother was diagnosed with cancer. I wish I had known the Lord then and knew what I know now; I feel as though that my mother would have beaten the disease. My sister away in college, and my mother did not want her to come home and I also wanted her to finish school. I couldn't leave.

The second time that he said come I couldn't leave I needed to care for my mother. As time went on of course she didn't get any better. On the third call to come she had only gotten worse and I still couldn't leave. By now a couple of years had passed, and he moved on. We slowly drifted apart. He was really the type of man that needs strong women by his side. So eventually he got married (it didn't lasts but he didn't get a divorce). I feel that I did the right thing and don't regret taking care of my mother. If I had to do it again I would do the same thing. My only regret is not crying and not begging him not to go.

It is amazing how satan arranges failures in your life. God has a plan for each one of us, and satan knows that plan and plans to destroy it. Satan puts together a plan long before you discover what God has planned for you.

(For I know the thoughts that I think toward for you, saith the Lord, thoughts of peace and not of evil, to give you an expected end. Jeremiah 29:11).

It seems, like everyone who has ever seen us together could sense that we were destined to be together. But years went by and little to no communication, only through family occasionally.

HOW I GOT TO THE MID-WEST!

*I*n the meantime my mother passed, and he had gotten married. My life down south had gone downhill, due to several circumstances surrounding me. I decided to move where he was. I knew that he was probably in a relationship which I had no intention to on interfering in, but I did want anyone to know where I had moved to. I had nothing and no family or friends there but him. I knew that he would assist me if needed.

I needed a fresh start. I told the Lord if He would get me out of the situation that I was involved in that I would serve Him. The Lord came to me and "Asked do you really want to leave?" I said Yes! Shortly after that a friend of mine called me and said that she would buy our tickets and she would get our luggage and she did. She had contacted a shelter and they were expecting us. This meant that I had to completely start over and really had to depend on God. I left the south with my 2 children, 200 dollars in food stamps and a little over $100 dollars in cash, 3 trunks, 3 bags and a suitcase and my purse. We got on the greyhound and never thought about returning to live. On the bus I heard satan say, "look at you, taking your children some where you don't know anyone but him, you have never been there before and don't know where you are going to stay or anything, just look at you. I responded well I guess I'll have to depend on the Lord! I only had a message phone number for him, when I got to one state away I called that number and Richard answered saying that he had been over to his apartment earlier that night, and he was going to return, and he would tell him I was coming, but when I get to the city to call him back. Then he said "that he had not had a drink (alcohol) in three years but he had been drinking all that night". He sounded pretty plastered at that time. I thought to myself that when I get there he would not be able to answer the phone. But I called him and he sent someone to pick us up from the bus station. When I got to Richards apartment he had a sign in the wall saying all phone calls were $.25 a call. I had the shelter's number and needed to call them. He allowed me to use the phone without a charge. When I called I was told that there was not any room but she gave me 13 other shelter numbers to call and If I didn't find space to call her back. I called all of them and none had space. I'm now stuck I didn't hear her say call back. But, I heard the Lord say "She said call her back!" so I did and she said "there was a lady leaving and I could have her space". She told me to get to the hospital and she would send a cab for us. Richard got us to the hospital and I only saw him again once or twice before he passed. I praise God for him and his connections. RIP, Thanks Richard!

When I got to the shelter it was a multiple story mansion,

A One-sided Always and Forever Love

simply beautiful. That night we had a <u>locking</u> room, access to a full and fully stocked kitchen, we had three twin size beds in our room, access to a washer and dryer, anything we needed from tooth paste to clothes, there was a play room for the children, outside play equipment for the children, fenced in, huge living room and dining room three or four full bathrooms. With lots of perks, tickets to the Zoo, movies, anything going on in the city at that time, free bus fair, you name it the shelter supplied it. Counsel, help with medical if needed. Of course there were rules that you had to follow, and promise not to tell anyone where they were located, being inside by a certain time. But look at GOD! (Jehovah Jirah, My Provider). They allowed you to live there 10 days, we stayed there 3 months. When I left the shelter I still had all of my money plus and food stamps plus, my trunks and luggage, my 2 children, but I had also 3 bed rooms of furniture, everything to stock my kitchen (pot, pans, silverware, plates...) living room furniture, dining room furniture, linen, curtains, including a nice color T.V. everything I needed to fill a 3 bed room, townhouse apartment free.

Section 8 (Federal housing) doesn't except applications for people all the time, it would only open occasionally, and some people would be on a waiting list for years. The day before I was leaving the shelter Section 8 opened up for applicants who qualified for what they called Federal Preference (Homeless). Living at the shelter on that day I was considered homeless. (Section 8 meant that I could move anywhere over the city, state or country with rent assistance. A big plus for me at that time it allowed me to choose the type of housing that I wanted practically anywhere. Again I say <u>"Look at God"</u>.)

(But my God will supply all your needs according to His riches in glory by Jesus Christ)

While I'm learning to like this city, he was hating it and deciding to move. When he approached me, I thought he was moving into the country and that was not me. So he left the city. We somewhat begin to loose contact again. Until his mother passed and we rode down together with our sons to her home going. It was a very intense drive. That's another whole story.

THE CLOSURE

*T*he death of his dad brought us back home again. He and my son rode with me back to our home town. But this time gave God a chance to pull this thing together. I got an opportunity to talk to him alone. I told him that I needed to say something to him. But I did not know how to say it. He asked if I was scared I said yes but I would get through it. Later, I mention that I needed closure. That I was stuck, he had moved on with his life and I could not. I decided that I would allow him to read a very small portion of this book. He read about 2 paragraphs and stood back and looked at me. (I was in the process of writing this book). I then asked if he remembered that particular incident. He said yes. I then I reminded him that we never broke up. We simply drifted apart. I really needed to finish a relationship before starting another one.

I still in my head always felt that someday we would get back together. Even though I knew that he had moved on I felted as though that the person in his life was just passing through as some have in my life. I have tried everything that I could to get over him and nothing has worked so I decided to go to the source and make a final breakup. I needed it spoken out loud, with no assumptions. It had to be final and completely parted. Our relationship officially defined. I need him to do it; I just was not strong enough. I never wanted the relationship to end. He has always been all that I wanted. I needed closure.

Well a day went by and he had a chance to think about it. He asked me to go for a ride with him. We rode across the bridge, it was a beautiful evening, the sky was clear. The weather was nice. Nice breeze. I was driving his truck another one of God's perfect days. We were just enjoying each other's company. Then he brought up the subject and his response was that I was a very good friend and the best friend that he ever had and would always be, he would always respect me for that and there was nothing the he would not do for me. Basically he loved me but not in love with me.

I thought that I would be distraught & hurt and crying so did he but, instead I was so relieved and it seemed like a weight lifted off my shoulders. My whole attitude changed, I finally exhaled. I felt my enter beauty emerge. My self-confidence arose. I felt like the old me had returned. I felt beautiful again. It was amazing the change that arose. I began to glow. I felt like a butterfly. I felt free. My joy returned, my happiness returned, peace surrounded me, I felt as though I was in love again but with myself. I saw him taking a second look at me my change was visible. It finally became all about me. My walk changed, the way I carried myself changed, I can't explain what all happen in that instance. I thought that I was going to be sad, instead I was excited.

Then the Lord brought back to mind a prophetic word that I had not long ago received.

(Which stated "the Lord said that He is in the process of finishing what He has begun, He said if I was ready to take the journey, He asked the question Are you ready to take the journey? The second leg of the trip, on the second leg of the trip He is going to take some turns and some twists and it might be a little bit different for you(me) it might be a little bit difficult. But what I want in this season of the journey is less arguing I want more of you to be the passenger. And to follow His lead, are you willing to do that my daughter? I am going to take you on a fantastic journey. And every time it gets difficult I want you to remind me God you said that you are taking me on a fantastic journey. When you mouth the words it is going to bring faith to your heart to hold on just like you hold on just like we might be on a roller coaster sometimes. But it is going to be a thrill of a lifetime. I promise you I am not tickling your emotions my daughter. I'm not going to tell you everything ahead of time, but if you trust me and go along for the ride I promise you will like the destination.)

I felt like I was a passenger on a fantastic journey and God was the conductor, it truly was a fantastic journey. I felt as though my husband will be able to find me now, I started being noticed again, one guy after another everywhere I went. Even he started noticing me again and keeping a "friendly" eye on me. I had test after test on this trip and I must say I passed maybe not with straight A's but high B's. I thank God for His mercy, grace, and guidance through it all. I had a fantastic time on this trip. A vacation anywhere else could not have been any better.

During the years I had a terrible illness. The doctors did not think that I would make it. But God had promised me total restoration. It is amazing to watch how God has healed and healed and restored and still restoring me on a daily basis. The doctors are always telling me something is wrong. But God heals it almost immediately (Jehovah Rophe, My healer). But He said total restoration. And it is happening. I PRAISE GOD!!!!

THEN CAME?

e returned to the mid-west. And eventually he moved back to the city where I now lived and we did keep in contact with each other. Things were good with me because I had my clear mind, soul, and heart.

My journey had not ended. I met and dated a couple of guys out of state in my travels. But they were not the one.

INTERNET DATING

I knew a couple of my friends that had met people on the internet, so I gave it a try. I did not expect anything to happen. I think I was looking for conversation more than anything. I went to a website called Black Planet. I put my picture in my profile with little information. Assuming that being black planet that I would meet black men. I was surprised that there were Caucasian men sending me messages (notes). Other hits were from very young Africans, Africans and American Indians. There were a number of instant messages. Mostly I ignored also. First I met Alex, tall, lighter skinned & what I called fine somewhat attractive man in Sweden. He told me he was an African that lived in Sweden and his mother was in Africa. He did not look African but, who am I to judge. His mother got sick and he decided to go back to Ghana to be with her and got stuck in Ghana and could not leave to go back to Sweden. He wanted me to come there but, I have no desire to go to Africa. That did not work. We talked for a minute and he claimed he could not find a job so we decided to start a business, he was to send me authentic African attire and I would sell it here in the states. Of course, he wanted me to invest the bulk of the funds. I refused to. (I don't give men money). Eventually he would be sending more African trinkets. Also he wanted to visit here, and asked me to invite him. I knew nothing about inviting, what would it take and what would be my responsibility? So I asked my Bishop. The first thing she said was are you sure this is him in this picture? He had sent so many pictures I said surely it must be him. But I did not know for sure. So I told him that I had talked to my bishop and she told me what to do, and he panic and decided to show me his real self. All I'm going to say is, he was nothing like the picture. Needless to say that was the end of that.

Well back to the internet. Browsing just to see who and what had hit on my page, there was another instant message (meaning that the person was on the internet at that moment and want to talk to me.) This time it was an American soldier. OMG! Sooo fine, very attractive, from Texas (you know everything grows big in Texas). In the army, serving time in Iraq & about to retire and looking for a wife and a mother for his 12yr old daughter, someone real, ready to settle down, travel and just enjoy life. He had so many pictures of him and his daughter. He had snap shots of Iraq and other soldiers. I even spoke with his daughter via email. He seems so excited to meet me with so many promises, and had built an entire life for us. He even proposed to me and wanted to move into one of his homes in New York. A world wind relationship for me that I deserve so much. The more we talked the more I liked him. It was almost too good to be true. But, I put God in everything therefore, if it was not right the Lord would stop it. The only thing about that is the flesh is weak and you have to be prepared for what God does. I don't believe that God would allow me to be destroyed. This is a part of my prayers.

My daughter asked me to send his picture and I did, she knew how to find out who was in the picture, if it was a scam. And guess what? Another African from Accra, Ghana had uploaded this man's pictures, pictures of his new born daughter, and his private home. Another scam! I praise the LORD His goodness and mercy, also for loving me more than I deserve. Both of these men live in Accra, Ghana. I am not one that gives men money, so all was to no prevail for them. Both of them had the same sad story. The second called himself Terry, both having no good wives that ran away with another man. This was my first and second experiences on the internet and I know that some people have successful relationships but, mine were disasters. And there are many other horrible stories. You have to keep praying, and believing that God will protect you, and will not guide you wrong. I told one of them did he really believe that God would allow him to hurt His daughter and not warn her. I'm so glad I know who and who's I am. I believe that God will supply your wants but He will expose what you are getting. He will warn you, you have to be aware conscious of His voice still and small, visions given, unnerving feelings, or something just that is not right. Then He allows you to make your choice.

WHERE IS HE?

My prayer was "God if it is not real or not true to tear it apart early before feelings are involved. Protect my heart and possessions, if it is not You. If it is You bless it my Lord in the name of Jesus" I truly believe that God answers my prayers, so I get ready for whatever happens. There are so many middle age women that are hungry for a companionship and affection and I am one of them. I want a successful relationship that will last forever. I have to believe that God has my best interest in the plan that He has written for me. I also pray that I don't miss what God has in store for me. Allow me to be open for to him. I feel that he will not be what I would normally choose for myself because; only God knows his heart and soul. OMG! Please allow me to recognize him, and give him a chance. Not look and see something small that I don't like and miss him.

Now I'm getting frustrated again, and telling God what I need and want in a man, more importantly asking for him to have what He wants for me in a man, adding wants as time moved on. I realized I need to be continuing to praying for my husband. Praying for his well-being, his health, wealth, finances, his Godliness and etc... (On the lighter side one of my wishes was, "I don't want anything old but money" Ha, ha, ha.) Because only God knew who he was and what was going on in his life.

Then I thought "Lord where is he?" I need to know that he exists. At least allow me to see him, to know that I wasn't chasing a dream or it being a figment of my imagination.

Joking around, I asked my ex- did he know a good man, who needs a good woman. You know that I am a good woman and need a good man. But I said, "I don't want anything old but money" & you fall in that group (meaning not him). He said I have this one friend, that just started staying with his mother to help her out and he mention his name. But that is all he said.

Then one day he call me saying that his car had caught on fire and he needed a ride home and asked me to pick him and a friend up. I said okay and I went to the location where he was. He does home repairs, remodeling and rehabbing houses. When I arrived, he and his friend were waiting. He forgot something and had to go back inside to get it and told his friend to get in the car. Well the young man was staring at me and didn't hear him. I rolled down the window and asked him was he going with us? He said "yes". I said you can get in I don't bite on Wednesday's. So he got in constantly staring at me. Not saying a word all the way to his house. When we arrived he got out and said "thank you".

Later, my ex told me that his friend asked him where did he meet a woman like that? How do you know her? He said that we used to date and we knew each other from childhood. I don't think he really thought about what the young man was saying or what he meant about his statement "Hummmm".

A few weeks later my landlord needed to make some repairs at my house and I recommended my ex to do the work. When he arrived, he brought the young man with him to help. When they arrived I open the door as he walked in, he looked into my eyes and said "I hoped I would see you again". It startled me for a second, because he was so much younger than me, and very attractive. I know that younger men were attracted to me and attractive men also, but I never worked with both, young and attractive. WOW! The whole time he was there he flirted with me. And you know I flirted back.

My ex had no idea that we were attracted to each other. He never saw between the lines or saw things growing and growing fast until it was too late to stop it. (It is funny when people say or do things not realizing what could really happen. His nose was so wide open thinking that I was so into him and I would not allow anyone else in and no one wanted me because I'm over 20years of celibacy, my age and size. Especially, since I got him the job at my house. He did not understand that I was truly free and I had all of me back, I'm whole again. Thank You Lord!!!) I asked him was this the friend he was talking about introducing to me. He said "yes". I asked do you know that this young man is the age of your son? He replied "you said you did not want anything old but money". He still had not realized that we were already connecting. My ex does not like plus size women, and I'm plus size (for now), and assumes that no other man should either. He knew that this man would not, mainly because he has watched him turn away so many nice looking (fine), and young women before. I truly thought that he thought that he would never say anything to me. He was trying to be funny.

When he realized that something was brewing with us, he started looking back into our relationship, friendship down through the years, and what and how we were together. All of my morals, standards, and personality, the over-all type of woman that I was and am, and now saved and sanctified. The way we prospered in such a short while together and of course my beauty and sweetness, and all the good times we had together. (All he had remembered before this moment was the bad things. I had to ask him was I a burden on you? Because of the stories he had to tell, nothing good or happy. The total opposite of what I was saying. But now to him they don't seem so bad and they were very few. It is amazing that two people in the same situation see things so very differently). Then he realized that I was the best woman he had ever had, he even said it aloud. As he re-lived the past he started talking about the good times and how things seemed to fall together for us. Life was really good and how happy he was during this time. (This made his friend second think of us getting together). It seemed like we belonged together, but I'm free. I'm released from the past and the hold he seem to have had over me. I don't want to be with him, I have nothing for him but maybe friendship and that is not necessary. I believe that now he wants to rekindle our relationship. But through the Grace of God I'm free. I did not realize the how heavy that burden it was on my mind, heart and soul. Lord I Thank You!!

When his friend understood that it was completely over him, he began to pursue me again. I had an age difference issue that I worked through but, strangely enough he seems to be okay with it from the beginning. I have a child older than him and one younger and very close to his age. I wrestled with it for a while, my oldest was okay but my youngest is very upset. My concern was what others would think, especially my children. I finally came to the conclusion that this is my life and if I'm happy and he treats me well, what was the problem? So I decided to go with it.

This man does all in his power to please me. He does what it takes to care for me. I have a number of medical problems and he is always there to give me assistance. He has made himself familiar with all of my problems and how to care for me. He does these things without being asked, full of care and love. He seems to enjoy it, and without being asked.

He is young enough and energetic for the simplest of things that are a real task for me. He always asking is there anything he can do for me, am I ok. One Sunday my pastor said to all the singles, to find out if your special friend can cook, clean, or sew, before you get too serious. Well, I chuckled to myself because he cooks & cleans, and had mention the day before that he would sew something that need repair. I thought that was funny.

We enjoy just sitting, talking and being in each other company. We enjoy lots of the same things, going to the same places and especially fishing. He told me on one of his fishing trips he was thinking and talking out loud. Saying "Lord I'm falling I love with this women. Is she the one? Just as he said that a large 12lb. catfish hit his line. He had not had a bite all day. After that happen a he said Lord is that a sign and another catfish larger than the last one hit his line. Well Lord it must be, THANK YOU LORD!

He makes me feel covered and protected as much as a human can. Of course nothing and no one covers us more and better than our Lord. My God is my greatest coverer and protector of all. As good as he is to me God is much greater in my life. Like I said as much as a human can.

I am a body person; some people are attracted to height, size, color and parts of the body and etc... But for me it is body design. I love his design. His arms are long enough. I never thought about it before but I'm a plus size women. Very few arms can surround my whole body and his does, being completely held. Plus size girls may understand what I'm saying.

I miss set on a stool and fell on the floor. He could not get to me before I got to the floor. But he came and attempted to lift me and before I could say anything he lifted me straight up off the floor and placed me on my feet. I did not think any human could pick me up like that. I'm well over 200lbs and he lifted me with little to no effort. (Plus size people may understand.) He totally blew me away. It is amazing how the Lord place people in position in your life when you need them, right time and the right place. It would have been very difficult to get up without his help.

One thing that I never thought about was height. I have dated short, average and extra tall men. I personally never wanted to look down on my man in any way. He is 6'1" just right I get to look up to him and continue to look up to my Lord. I mean that I see both of them looking in the same direction. I personally like that.

He constantly confesses his feelings for me, as well as showing it in the open, telling his parents and close friends first. Then on his Facebook page. He doesn't care who is watching. He is God fearing man. He is very generous financially. He shows an interest in what I'm interested in. He loves children and pets and they love him. I feel that God really out did Himself when He placed us together. I am so comfortable with him.

He said that he asked God for a good woman and there I was. I do feel that God placed us together. I could not figure why my ex was still in my life and in my way for so long. I thought God had me praying and lifting him up for him. But God used him as an avenue for us to meet. I met this man through him, so we would get a chance to meet and get to know each other. If I passed him in the street, at a party or at church, I never would have given him a conversation. I never would have believed that he would be interested in me, or I never would have considered him to be a life time mate. I doubt I would have even said hello. My mom always said that the Lord works in mysterious ways, using the friendship with my ex as an avenue for us to meet. He seems to be at least 80% of what I wanted in a man but it is growing more and more each day. Understand no one is 100% of what you want mainly because all you want is not God's will. Everything you experience there is a reason behind it. You have to except what God, GOD, **GOD** gives you because He knows what you want, need, what is best for you and it may not be in the package you expect.

There are so many small things that make us fit together, that only God would have produced. (And there are something's that we will grow together.) In my prayers before we met was "Lord was where's the man that you made, to fit me and me to fit him?" God answers prayers. Although there will be times you think that you are alone just know He will never leave you of forsake you (Jehovah Shammah, Omni Present). Some of the things that I have notice: he is tall enough, his arms long enough to hold me tight, he is thick enough; I never liked thin men because of my size. I felt that they could not pick me up. He looks at me as if he could sopped me up with a biscuit ha, ha, ha. When he looks at me his whole face smiles and lightens up, he is kind, and thoughtful, caring, he is man enough, when he touches me oh so gentle & caring along with a handsome smile. His hands are heavy enough that makes me feel secure. I always feel so special. I think he is a very good man and I thank the Lord for him.

And to top all with in the second month of meeting me he told all of his family and friends that he was going to marry me. They knew before I knew he was considering it. When a man finds who he wants it does not take him all day, a year, or 2 years to know for sure. And he will move on it. I heard someone say, "If you have been with someone more than a year and he has not at least talked about marriage. He is with you until he finds someone better. Above all stay tuned in with the Lord! Well, we will see if marriage is there!!! Oh did I say I think I Love Him!